71599665

W9-BGB-809

LEVEL 2

Animals in the City

Elizabeth Carney

NATIONAL GEOGRAPHIC

Washington, D.C.

To my daughter, Eleanora, who explores the wilds of Brooklyn with me with enthusiasm and wonder
—E. C.

Published by National Geographic Partners, LLC, Washington, D.C. 20036. All rights reserved. Reproduction in whole or in part without written permission of the publisher is prohibited.

NATIONAL GEOGRAPHIC and Yellow Border Design are trademarks of the National Geographic Society, used under license.

Designed by Yay! Design

Library of Congress Cataloging-in-Publication Data

Names: Carney, Elizabeth, 1981- author. | National Geographic Kids (Firm), publisher. | National Geographic Society (U.S.)
Title: Animals in the city / by Beth Carney.
Description: Washington, DC : National Geographic Kids, [2019] | Series: National geographic readers | Audience: Age 5-8. | Audience: K to Grade 3.
Identifiers: LCCN 2018036069 (print) | LCCN 2018039024 (ebook) | ISBN 9781426333330 (e-book) | ISBN 9781426333316 (paperback) | ISBN 9781426333323 (hardcover)
Subjects: LCSH: Urban animals--Juvenile literature. | Urban ecology (Biology)--Juvenile literature. | City and town life--Juvenile literature.
Classification: LCC QL49 (ebook) | LCC QL49 .C287 2019 (print) | DDC 591.9173/2--dc23
LC record available at https://lccn.loc.gov/2018036069

The author and publisher gratefully acknowledge the expert content review of this book by Suzanne MacDonald, Ph.D., professor of psychology, specializing in comparative cognition and animal behavior, York University, Toronto, Canada; and by Catherine Workman, senior director, Wildlife, National Geographic Society; and the literacy review of this book by Mariam Jean Dreher, professor of reading education, University of Maryland, College Park.

Author's Note
The cover of this book features a pigeon high up on a city building, and the title page shows a mountain lion prowling the Hollywood Hills of California, U.S.A. The table of contents has an image of a red squirrel holding a walnut.

Photo Credits
GI = Getty Images; NGC = National Geographic Creative; SS = Shutterstock
Cover, Mettus/SS; 1, Steve Winter/NGC; 3, photomaster/SS; 5, Sean Pavone/SS; 6, Edwin Giesbers/Nature Picture Library; 7, Marino Todesco/EyeEm/GI; 8, Luke Massey/Nature Picture Library; 10, Dr. Stanley D Gehrt/NGC; 11, Thomas Kitchin/Design Pics Inc/Alamy Stock Photo; 12, Don Johnston/Alamy Stock Photo; 14 (1), Bernard Guillas; 14 (2), Mark MacEwen/Nature Picture Library; 14 (3), Eric Isselée/SS; 15 (4), Steve Winter/NGC; 15 (5), Anan Kaewkhammul/SS; 15 (6), Ian Wade Photography/GI; 16, David Coleman/Dreamstime; 17, Eric Isselée/SS; 18, Franz-Marc Frei/GI; 19, Oliver Smart/Alamy Stock Photo; 20-21, Cyril Ruoso/Minden Pictures; 22 (UP), Denja1/GI; 22 (LO), Paolo Cocco/AFP/GI; 23, Frances Roberts/Alamy Stock Photo; 25 (UP LE), Joel Sartore/NGC; 25 (UP RT), Alizada Studios/SS; 25 (background), Lisa Johnson - Olive Productions/GI; 26, Roy Toft/NGC; 27, Jan Sochor/Latincontent/GI; 28-29, Clark Stevens/Raymond Garcia for Resource Conservation District of the Santa Monica Mountains; 29, Razvan Ciuca/GI; 30 (1), Derek Middleton/Minden Pictures; 30 (2), Johncarnemolla/Dreamstime; 30 (3 UP), Michael Conrad/SS; 30 (3 LE), Alan Tunnicliffe/SS; 30 (3 RT), dangdumrong/SS; 30 (3 LO), Cynthia Kidwell/SS; 31 (4), Holger Ehlers/SS; 31 (5), Eric Slezak/EyeEm/GI; 31 (6), Steve Winter/NGC; 31 (7), Kike Calvo/NGC; 32 (UP LE), Luke Massey/Nature Picture Library; 32 (UP RT), Robyn Mackenzie/Dreamstime; 32 (CTR LE), Ana Gram/SS; 32 (CTR RT), Jan Sochor/Latincontent/GI; 32 (LO LE), Marino Todesco/EyeEm/GI; 32 (LO RT), alexmisu/SS; Top border (throughout), hugolacasse/SS; Vocabulary box art, Sudowoodo/SS

**National Geographic supports K–12 educators with ELA Common Core Resources.
Visit natgeoed.org/commoncore for more information.**

Table of Contents

Wild Cities

Streetlights. Traffic. Crowded crosswalks. We're used to seeing cities packed with people.

But have you noticed that cities are full of animals, too? What animals would you expect to see in a city?

Pigeons (PIJ-unz) are a common
sight in many cities. They might
start their day strolling through
a park. They peck birdseed that
people feed them.

Later, they might strut down a busy street, looking for bits of dropped food. Like many city animals, pigeons are scavengers. They find plenty to eat in a city.

Talk of the Town

SCAVENGER: An animal that survives by finding plants, dead animals, or trash to eat

This peregrine (PER-uh-grin) falcon mother built her nest in a planter on a city balcony.

Many types of animals choose to live in cities. It's easy for them to find food there, so they move in.

Other animals don't have a choice. As humans push into wild places, many animals lose their natural homes. They must learn to adapt to their new surroundings.

Let's meet some other recently spotted city critters!

Talk of the Town

ADAPT: To change in order to survive in different conditions

New Neighbors

In Chicago, a stadium parking lot holds a secret. There, a mother coyote (kye-YOH-tee) raises her cubs in a hidden den. About 2,000 coyotes live in Chicago.

A coyote sits in a parking lot outside Soldier Field in Chicago.

Coyotes that live in a city may raid trash cans to find food.

Crafty coyotes are well suited to city living. Why? They'll eat almost anything. And they use their smarts to stay safe while getting around the city.

Imagine finding a 300-pound black bear digging through your trash can! Or suppose you saw one swiping birdseed from a backyard bird feeder!

In many suburbs across North America, run-ins like these are becoming more common. That's because bears often go where it's easy for them to find food.

Talk of the Town

SUBURB: An area of homes and businesses found just outside a city

6 AMAZING City Sightings

A sea lion pup wanders into a seaside restaurant in San Diego, California, U.S.A.

1

2

In Jaipur, India, rhesus macaques (REE-sus muh-KAKS) sometimes raid food markets.

3

A wild boar stumbles into a shopping mall in Hong Kong.

4

A mountain lion prowls through the Hollywood Hills in Los Angeles, California.

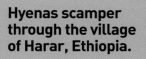

5

Hyenas scamper through the village of Harar, Ethiopia.

6

Red foxes dart through parking lots in Bristol, England.

City Smarts

City raccoons are better at problem-solving than country raccoons.

Some city animals learn surprising new skills that help them succeed at city living.

In an experiment, 22 city raccoons and 22 country raccoons were given a puzzle. They had to break into a garbage can to get the food inside. But the garbage can was held closed with a cord. None of the country raccoons could open the can. But most of the city raccoons could!

Many kinds of birds have figured out clever ways to find food in the city, too. In Barbados (bar–BAY–dohs), some bullfinches steal sugar packets off restaurant tables. They peck a hole in the packets to score a sweet treat.

Outdoor restaurants like this one often attract birds that are looking for food.

The Barbados bullfinch lives only on the island of Barbados.

Too Close for Comfort?

Sometimes, wild animals and people can clash in cities. In Cape Town, South Africa, baboons have been known to break into homes to raid people's cupboards. They'll even swipe food from people walking down the street.

Some cities have major bird poop problems. Every year, millions of starlings fly through Rome, Italy, as they migrate. And where there are birds, there's bird poop!

starling

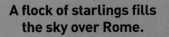

A flock of starlings fills the sky over Rome.

In New York City, pigeon poop often lands on parked cars.

Poop-covered streets can become so slippery that cars skid off the road. In New York City, pigeons release more than 25 million pounds of poop each year. Yuck!

Talk of the Town

MIGRATE: To move from one place to another at a certain time of year

Run-ins with wild animals can sometimes be dangerous— for people and for the animals.

In Australia, people have moved into much of the koala's habitat. Now koalas are more likely to get hurt. As a result, special hospitals have been set up to treat injured koalas.

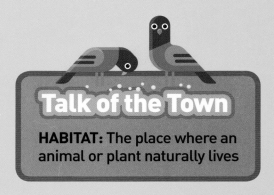

Talk of the Town

HABITAT: The place where an animal or plant naturally lives

Signs warn drivers to use caution on roads that pass through areas where koalas live.

Special ambulances bring injured koalas to the hospital.

Scientists are studying how animals adapt to city living. In Brazil, for example, marmosets have moved into city parks. In the city, the marmosets meet a predator they don't see in their natural habitat—pet cats! Scientists want to know how city marmosets stay safe from them. Learning about how city animals live can help keep both people and animals safe.

Marmosets are tiny monkeys that usually live in rain forest treetops.

Talk of the Town

PREDATOR: An animal that hunts and eats other animals

Living Together

People are finding new ways to share space peacefully with wildlife. In Los Angeles, there are plans to build a wildlife bridge across a busy freeway. The bridge will help mountain lions and other animals move safely through their habitat.

This image shows what the Liberty Canyon Wildlife Crossing will look like once it's built.

You can safely share space, too! Follow these tips: Don't feed wild animals. Keep your distance. Be sure your pets are inside at night. Put bells on cats' collars to keep birds safe. Use animal-proof garbage cans. With care, humans and animals can live as good neighbors.

QUIZ WHIZ

How much do you know about animals that live in cities?
After reading this book, probably a lot! Take this quiz and find out.
Answers are at the bottom of page 31.

1

What does a scavenger eat?

A. only freshly killed meat
B. plants, dead animals, or trash
C. only plants
D. only fish

2

What have people in Australia done to help injured koalas?

A. They planted eucalyptus trees.
B. They trained koala-sniffing dogs.
C. They set up special hospitals.
D. They built koala-proof trash cans.

Which could be an example of an animal adapting to city living?

3

A. An owl finds rodents beneath snow.
B. A squirrel hides acorns in small burrows.
C. A tiger sharpens its claws on a tree.
D. A hawk hunts pigeons instead of its usual prey.

4

What item might help keep raccoons away from human food?

A. animal-proof garbage cans
B. sensors
C. raccoon-proof cars
D. video cameras

5

How much pigeon poop falls on New York City every year?

A. 5,000 pounds
B. 1 million pounds
C. 15 million pounds
D. 25 million pounds

6

The wildlife bridge in Los Angeles will help animals safely cross _____.

A. a river
B. an amusement park
C. a lake
D. a freeway

Which predator do city marmosets meet that they don't see in their natural habitat?

A. coyotes
B. jaguars
C. pet cats
D. pythons

7

Answers: 1. B; 2. C; 3. D; 4. A; 5. D; 6. D; 7. C

ADAPT: To change in order to survive in different conditions

HABITAT: The place where an animal or plant naturally lives

MIGRATE: To move from one place to another at a certain time of year

PREDATOR: An animal that hunts and eats other animals

SCAVENGER: An animal that survives by finding plants, dead animals, or trash to eat

SUBURB: An area of homes and businesses found just outside a city